Ext 3 0050 05425 4148

j 569.31 Gra

DISCARD

DATE DUE

DEMCO, INC. 38-2931

This Material is Donated
by a Grant from

SCOTT COUNTY
REGIONAL
AUTHORITY

with Gaming Tax Dollars
provided from
Isle of Capri Casino
Bettendorf, IA

D1060754

MAR 1 1 2005

DAVENPORT PUBLIC LIBRARY
DAVENPORT, IOWA 52801-1490

EXPLORING DINOSAURS & PREHISTORIC CREATURES

GLYPTODONTS

By Susan H. Gray

THE CHILD'S WORLD®
CHANHASSEN, MINNESOTA

The Child's World®

Published in the United States of America by The Child's World®
PO Box 326, Chanhassen, MN 55317-0326
800-599-READ
www.childsworld.com

*Content Adviser:
Brian Huber, PhD,
Curator, Department
of Paleobiology,
Smithsonian
National Museum
of Natural History,
Washington DC*

Photo Credits: Illustration by Karen Carr: 24; Robert Pickett/Corbis: 9; Theo Allofs/Corbis: 15; Gianni Dagli Orti/Corbis: 25; Dean Conger/Corbis: 26; The Field Museum, GEO84482c: 5; The Field Museum, CK20T, Photographer Ron Testa: 17; Mike Fredericks: 7, 13; Roger Viollet/Getty Images: 20; Michael Long/The Natural History Museum, London: 6; The Natural History Museum, London: 8, 21, 27; Orbis/The Natural History Museum, London: 12; John Sibbick/The Natural History Museum, London: 22; Samuel R. Maglione/Photo Researchers, Inc: 11; Tom McHugh/Natural History Museum of L.A. County/Photo Researchers, Inc.: 18; From the Collections of the Texas Memorial Museum, The University of Texas at Austin, Glyptotherium floridanum (TMM 30967-1926): 19.

The Child's World®: Mary Berendes, Publishing Director

Editorial Directions, Inc.: E. Russell Primm, Editorial Director; Pam Rosenberg, Line Editor; Katie Marsico, Associate Editor; Matthew Messbarger, Editorial Assistant; Susan Hindman, Copy Editor; Melissa McDaniel, Proofreader; Tim Griffin/IndexServ, Indexer; Olivia Nellums, Fact Checker; Dawn Friedman, Photo Researcher; Linda S. Koutris, Photo Selector

Original cover art by Todd Marshall

The Design Lab: Kathleen Petelinsek, Design; Kari Thornborough, Page Production

Copyright © 2005 by The Child's World®
All rights reserved. No part of this book may be reproduced or utilized in any form or by any means without written permission from the publisher.

Library of Congress Cataloging-in-Publication Data
Gray, Susan Heinrichs.
  Glyptodonts / by Susan H. Gray.
    p. cm. — (Exploring dinosaurs & prehistoric creatures)
  Includes index.
  ISBN 1-59296-408-7 (lib. bd. : alk. paper) 1. Glyptodontidae—Juvenile literature. I. Title.
  QE882.E2G69 2005
  569'.31—dc22   2004018070

TABLE OF CONTENTS

CHAPTER ONE

A SORE LOSER

It had finally come to this. The two male glyptodonts (GLIP-tuh-dawnts) stood facing each other on a hilltop. They just couldn't share the same territory any longer. They were always getting in each other's way. Whenever one would find a great place to feed, the other would barge in. Soon they'd be competing for the same females. One of them had to go.

The two butted each other with their blocky heads, but neither one backed off. Then the smaller animal shoved his domed shell against the larger one. The bigger glyptodont stumbled a few steps backward and turned away. The smaller animal sensed victory and relaxed. Then, all of a sudden, WHACK! The big glyptodont's tail slammed into the small glyptodont's side and knocked him over.

A glyptodont feeds peacefully but, if another glyptodont comes near, he may need to fight to defend his territory.

In fact, it knocked him so hard that he began rolling down

the hill. Over and over he tumbled, until he landed at the bottom.

Unfortunately, he landed on his back, with his stubby legs in the air.

The glyptodont rocked back and forth.

Glyptodonts resembled modern-day armadillos but were much larger. Their size and bulky shells would have made it hard for these creatures to right themselves if they toppled over.

This was not good. The animal pressed his head against the ground. He pushed his tail into the dirt. He kicked his chunky legs. Finally, he tumbled over one more time and landed on his feet. The glyptodont was aching and sore. But at least he had survived the contest and the tumble. He waddled off, looking for a new place to live.

CHAPTER TWO

WHAT WERE THE GLYPTODONTS?

Glyptodonts were huge animals that were about the size of a small car. They lived from about 40 million to 10,000 years ago. The name *glyptodont* comes from Greek words meaning "carved tooth." This refers to the grooves that ran down the sides of the glyptodonts' teeth.

Glyptodonts walked on four short, stocky legs. The front legs ended in feet with sharp claws. The

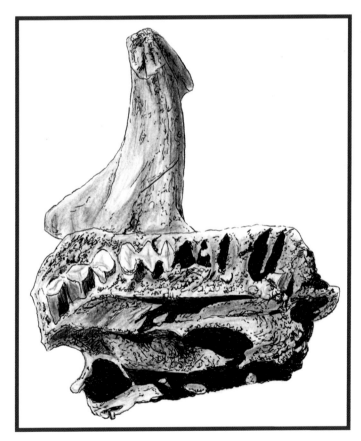

Scientists can study the jaws of glyptodonts to learn more about their teeth and eating habits.

back feet also were clawed, but sometimes these claws were thick and dull. Glyptodonts had heavy, muscular tails covered with bony armor. If the animals needed to defend themselves,

Glyptodonts had bony tails that could be used as powerful and dangerous weapons.

they could whip their tails around with great force.

Each glyptodont had a tall, domed shell that covered its back, neck, and sides. In the largest animals, the shell was about 5 feet (1.5 meters) tall and 6 feet (1.8 m) wide. Shells were made up of hundreds of many-sided plates that were fused together. The plates—

often called scutes (SKOOTS)—were 2 inches (5 centimeters) thick in some places. Such thick plates made the shell extremely heavy, maybe even more than 1,000 pounds (454 kilograms) in the larger animals.

The glyptodont had a helmet of bony armor protecting its head. It had a short, deep skull, a massive jawbone, and strong chewing muscles. The front of the mouth was toothless, but farther back there were many stout teeth for grinding.

GLYPTODON CLAVIPES

The glyptodonts were related to the living armadillos but were very much bigger. They were more heavily armoured than any other four-legged animal of Pleistocene times.

The carapace, composed of many thick polygonal plates of bone, covered the whole of the animal's body; the head too was covered by a thick bony shield and was completely protected when tucked in. The large armoured tail, the form of which varied between species, was probably employed as a powerful weapon. The glyptodonts were plant-eaters and may have used their claws to dig for roots and tubers.

While a glyptodont's dome-shaped shell didn't make it the most graceful of animals, the armor was an excellent defense against **predators.**

CHAPTER THREE

WHAT'S IT LIKE TO LIVE IN A DOME?

What was it like to live inside a big shell as the glyptodonts did? The shell, or carapace (CARE-uh-pace), must have been a big part of the glyptodont's life. It affected how the animal moved, ate, fought, and grew.

The carapace hung over the glyptodont's neck. The animal could not look up or to the sides very far because its head bumped into its shell. The heavy carapace also kept the glyptodonts close to the ground. Like turtles, they had no way to rear up on their hind legs to feed or look around. Their shape, balance, and weight would not allow it.

A glyptodont could not wiggle around much inside its shell. Its backbones were fused together into a stiff rod. A few separate neck bones gave the animal a little **flexibility.** The hip bones

Like a prehistoric glyptodont, this modern-day box turtle is not able to rear up on its hind legs.

were attached to the inside of the carapace and could not swing

back and forth.

In order to support the heavy weight of the shell, glyptodonts

had thick leg and foot bones and chunky limbs. Such legs are not

Because of their shape and body structure, glyptodonts were slow, clumsy animals.

the best for running, so glyptodonts must have been slow-moving

animals. They were not very **agile,** either. The animals could not turn

quickly, and they could not turn around in a small space. Nor could

they climb up and down steep hillsides. If glyptodonts battled one

another, it was probably a pretty slow event. Except when swinging

their muscular tails, their movements were not exactly lightning fast.

At birth, the glyptodont shell was leathery, lightweight, and soft. The scutes were not yet hardened, and the weight was not much of a burden. Therefore, as babies, the glyptodonts were probably more flexible, energetic, and active than at any other time of their lives. With age, the scutes became thicker, harder, and heavier. As the young glyptodonts grew, they developed the huge bones and strong muscles needed to support their heavy shells.

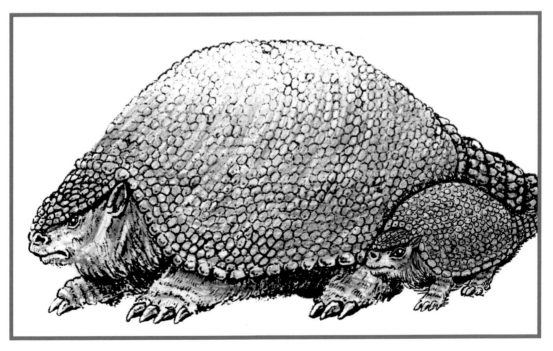

A young glyptodont looked a lot like an adult glyptodont, only smaller.

THE GLYPTODONTS' RELATIVES

Scientists tell us that glyptodonts, anteaters (right), sloths, and armadillos are related. But what do these animals have in common? It can't be their looks. Glyptodonts looked like igloos with legs. Anteaters are much smaller animals with long, drawn-out faces. Sloths have long hairy arms and legs. Armadillos look like scaly reptiles.

Still, these animals do have some things in common. For one thing, all of these animals are mammals (MAM-ulz). This means that they have hair or fur on their bodies. It also means that their babies are born alive instead of hatching from eggs. Anteaters and sloths are quite furry animals, and even armadillos have hair on their bellies. The glyptodonts may not have been very furry, but they probably did have some short, coarse hairs on their heads, shells, legs, and undersides.

Anteaters, sloths, and armadillos share something else with the glyptodonts: They all have unusual joints in their backbones. Joints are the places where two bones meet or rub together. The backbones are stacked together in a row. In most

mammals, each backbone rubs the next one in the row at certain points. In glyptodonts, anteaters, sloths, and armadillos, some bones rub together at two extra points. In other words, these animals have extra joints in their backs.

Because of their joints, scientists have given this group of animals a special name—xenarthrans (zen-AR-thrunz). *Xenarthran* comes from Greek words that mean "strange joint." Xenarthrans have other things in common, too. They either have no teeth or they have peglike teeth. They are not fierce predators. Most xenarthrans eat insects or plant matter. They also have small brains for the size of their bodies.

Clearly, related animals don't always have to look alike. Scientists who study their bodies and habits often find hidden similarities.

CHAPTER FOUR

How Did Glyptodonts Spend Their Time?

Glyptodonts probably spent their time doing everything slowly. With heavy shells to lug around, they weren't fast movers, and they didn't cover a lot of territory in a day. Scientists believe that they ambled around in low-lying areas, not far from water sources such as lakes or streams.

The glyptodonts spent some part of every day eating. The grasses, ferns, and bushes that existed in their time were similar to those that grow today. The animals fed mainly on plant stems and leaves. They may also have used their clawed hands for digging up roots. In general, xenarthrans do not burn calories or use energy very quickly. So glyptodonts probably did not have to eat as much as some other huge animals did.

*A young glyptodont (far right) stayed with its mother
until it was ready to digest plant matter.*

Females did not lay eggs, but gave birth to live babies. Little

glyptodonts had soft, flexible shells made up of tiny scutes. They drank

milk from their mothers until their little teeth and stomachs were

ready to handle plants. Throughout life, their teeth grew continu-

ously because tough plant material was always wearing them down.

Despite their armored shells, it is possible that glyptodonts had to be on the lookout for predators such as saber-toothed cats (right).

Scientists do not know a lot about the glyptodonts' enemies.

Perhaps with their huge, protective shells, glyptodonts traveled and

slept safely anywhere. On the other hand, maybe large predators

went after the giant animals or flipped them over to bite their

softer undersides.

CHAPTER FIVE

SOME DIFFERENT GLYPTODONTS

Although the different glyptodonts looked basically the same, they were not exactly alike. *Glyptotherium* (GLIP-toh-THIR-ee-um) lived in South America and in the warm, southernmost parts of North America. It weighed as much as a ton and walked with slow, heavy steps. From snout to tail tip, an adult was about 10 feet (3 m) in length.

By studying these Glyptotherium *remains, scientists can solve the mysteries of the past. Fossils provide clues about everything from how an animal moved to what it ate.*

Most of the Glyptodon *fossils now on display at museums were originally uncovered in South American countries such as Argentina.*

Glyptodon (GLIP-toh-dawn) lived in South America. In addition to its body armor, *Glyptodon* had a helmet of armor for its head and rings of armor on its short, thick tail. It was about the same size as *Glyptotherium.*

Doedicurus (dee-dih-KYOO-russ) was another South American glyptodont. Adults often grew to be 13 feet (4 m) in length.

Doedicurus may have weighed more than a ton, with at least half of that weight in the shell.

Doedicurus had one other outstanding feature—its mighty tail. Almost as long as the rest of the body, the tail was flexible and ringed with bony armor. At the end, the tail expanded into a club loaded with sharp spikes. *Doedicurus* could swing its tail with incredible force and probably did so to fend off attackers. A male may also have used its tail to whack other males that competed with it for food, space, or mates.

Although Doedicurus *was a mammal, its tail (shown here) was similar to that of a dinosaur called* Ankylosaurus *(AN-kuh-low-SAWR-uhss). Both animals had clubs on their tails that were used to fend off attackers.*

THE BRIDGE THAT CHANGED EVERYTHING

About 5 million years ago, the ancestors of bears, horses, dogs, cats,

and raccoons roamed throughout North America. At the same time, South America was home to armadillos, opossums, porcupines, and giant ground sloths (left). The animals of the two continents were in worlds of their own. They never wandered into one another's territory. They never competed for food or space. They never even saw each other. This was because the two landmasses were separated by a wide stretch of ocean. Each continent had its own plants and animals.

But something was happening that would change everything. Huge sections of Earth's crust, called plates, were shifting, and the landmasses were shifting with them. The movement was so slow that it could not be seen or felt. As the plates moved around, some landforms slowly disappeared into the ocean, some rose up from the sea, and some simply changed position.

In time, a strip of land appeared between North and South America. It connected the two continents by forming a land bridge between them. Once the land bridge was in place, South American animals could make their way into North America. Armadillos, porcupines, ground sloths, and other creatures slowly moved into the areas we know as Mexico and the United States. In the meantime, bears, horses, and other North American animals slowly traveled into South American lands.

Glyptodonts were among the South American animals that moved north. It took centuries for these creatures to spread into their new area. But in time, they made it as far east as Florida and as far west as Arizona. Thanks to the land bridge, people in the United States are finding glyptodont remains today.

CHAPTER SIX

WHAT BECAME OF THE GLYPTODONTS?

The glyptodonts were certainly well-protected animals. They had terrific armor, even on their heads and tails. Because they lived near lakes or rivers, they had plenty of water. There was

Glyptodonts shared their habitat with many other creatures, but there was plenty of room for all of them and enough food and water to go around.

Mammoths were elephant-like creatures that lived at the same time as glyptodonts. Scientists have uncovered their fossils in Asia, Europe, and North America.

no shortage of space for them to spread out, especially after the land bridge formed. So what became of these beasts? Why aren't they still with us today?

We know the glyptodonts died out at about the same time that many other animals did. The glyptodonts shared Earth with fearsome saber-toothed cats. They lived at the same time as the mighty mammoths. They roamed freely across the same lands as the giant ground sloths. But all of these other animals died out, too.

It could be that changes in climate led to their disappearance. The climate is the overall weather in a large area. About 10,000 years ago, the climate was changing. An ice age was ending, and Earth was starting to warm up. Ice sheets covering the lands farthest north and south were melting, and sea levels were rising. Plants that lived in warm areas sprang up everywhere, while cold-climate plants died.

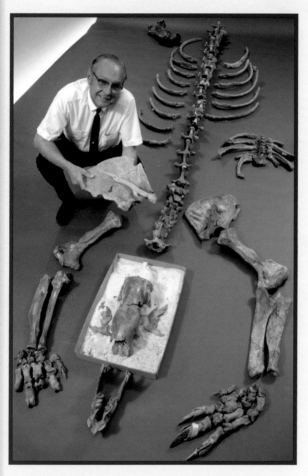

A scientist studies the remains of a giant ground sloth. These creatures were related to South America's modern-day tree sloths.

Once temperatures rose and ice sheets began to melt, new plant life developed on Earth. This may have affected the glyptdonts' food supply and caused the prehistoric mammals to die out.

Perhaps things were changing too fast for the glyptodonts.

Maybe their favorite plants were becoming harder to find. It is

possible that they could not handle the warmer temperatures.

Whatever the reason, the glyptodonts were unable to survive

the changes, and one by one, they disappeared.

Glossary

agile (AJ-ile) Something that is agile is able to move quickly and gracefully. Scientists do not believe that glyptodonts were agile animals.

ancestors (AN-sess-turz) Relatives who lived in the past are your ancestors. About 5 million years ago, the ancestors of bears, horses, dogs, cats, and raccoons made their homes in North America.

continents (KON-tuh-nuhnts) The great landmasses of the Earth are called continents. Several million years ago, a land bridge formed and connected the continents of North America and South America.

flexibility (fleks-uh-BIL-uh-tee) Flexibility is the ability to bend easily. Glyptodonts had a little flexibility in their necks.

predators (PRED-uh-torz) Predators are animals that hunt and eat other animals. Xenarthrans are not predators.

reptiles (REP-tilez) Reptiles are air-breathing animals that have a backbone and are usually covered with scales or plates. Armadillos look similar to scaly reptiles.

sloths (SLAWTHS) Sloths are furry, slow-moving animals. Sloths are related to glyptodonts.

Did You Know?

▸ Glyptodont remains have been found as far south as Antarctica.

▸ Some glyptodont shells had more than 1,000 scutes.

▸ The land bridge connecting North America and South America is not the only one that ever existed. Another land bridge once connected Russia and Alaska, allowing cold-climate animals to pass back and forth.

How to Learn More

AT THE LIBRARY

Lambert, David, Darren Naish, and Liz Wyse. *Dinosaur Encyclopedia: From Dinosaurs to the Dawn of Man.* New York: Dorling Kindersley, 2001.

Palmer, Douglas, and Barry Cox (editor). *The Simon & Schuster Encyclopedia of Dinosaurs & Prehistoric Creatures: A Visual Who's Who of Prehistoric Life.* New York: Simon & Schuster, 1999.

ON THE WEB

Visit our home page for lots of links about glyptodonts:

http://www.childsworld.com/links.html

NOTE TO PARENTS, TEACHERS, AND LIBRARIANS: We routinely verify our Web links to make sure they're safe, active sites—so encourage your readers to check them out!

PLACES TO VISIT OR CONTACT

AMERICAN MUSEUM OF NATURAL HISTORY
To view numerous fossils and learn more about prehistoric creatures
Central Park West at 79th Street
New York, NY 10024-5192
212/769-5100

CARNEGIE MUSEUM OF NATURAL HISTORY
To view a variety of fossils
4400 Forbes Avenue
Pittsburgh, PA 15213
412/622-3131

SMITHSONIAN NATIONAL MUSEUM OF NATURAL HISTORY
To see several fossil exhibits and take special behind-the-scenes tours
10th Street and Constitution Avenue NW
Washington, DC 20560-0166
202/357-2700

The Geologic Time Scale

CAMBRIAN PERIOD

Date: 540 million to 505 million years ago
Most major animal groups appeared by the
end of this period. Trilobites were common
and algae became more diversified.

ORDOVICIAN PERIOD

Date: 505 million to 440 million years ago
Marine life became more diversified. Crinoids
and blastoids appeared, as did corals and
primitive fish. The first land plants appeared.
The climate changed greatly during this period—it began as warm and moist, but temperatures ultimately dropped. Huge glaciers
formed, causing sea levels to fall.

SILURIAN PERIOD

Date: 440 million to 410 million years ago
Glaciers melted, sea levels rose, and Earth's
climate became more stable. Plants with
vascular systems developed. This means they
had parts that helped them to conduct food
and water.

DEVONIAN PERIOD

Date: 410 million to 360 million years ago
Fish became more diverse, as did land plants.
The first trees and forests appeared at this
time, and the earliest seed-bearing plants began
to grow. The first land-living vertebrates and
insects appeared. Fossils also reveal evidence
of the first ammonoids and amphibians. The
climate was warm and mild.

CARBONIFEROUS PERIOD

Date: 360 million to 286 million years ago
The climate was warm and humid, but
cooled toward the end of the period. Coal
swamps dotted the landscape, as did a
multitude of ferns. The earliest reptiles
appeared on Earth. Pelycosaurs such as
Edaphosaurus evolved toward the end
of the Carboniferous period.

PERMIAN PERIOD

Date: 286 million to 248 million years ago
Algae, sponges, and corals were common
on the ocean floor. Amphibians and reptiles
were also prevalent at this time, as were
seed-bearing plants and conifers. This period
ended with the largest mass extinction on
Earth. This may have been caused by volcanic
activity or the formation of glaciers and the
lowering of sea levels.

TRIASSIC PERIOD

Date: 248 million to 208 million years ago
The climate during this period was warm
and dry. The first true mammals appeared,
as did frogs, salamanders, and lizards. Ever-
green trees made up much of the plant life.
The first dinosaurs, including *Coelophysis*,
existed on Earth. In the skies, pterosaurs
became the earliest winged reptiles to
take flight. In the seas, ichthyosaurs and
plesiosaurs made their appearance.

JURASSIC PERIOD

Date: 208 million to 144 million years ago

The climate of the Jurassic period was warm and moist. The first birds appeared at this time, and plant life was more diverse and widespread. Although dinosaurs didn't even exist in the beginning of the Triassic period, they ruled Earth by Jurassic times. *Allosaurus, Apatosaurus, Archaeopteryx, Brachiosaurus, Compsognathus, Diplodocus, Ichthyosaurus, Plesiosaurus,* and *Stegosaurus* were just a few of the prehistoric creatures that lived during this period.

CRETACEOUS PERIOD

Date: 144 million to 65 million years ago

The climate of the Cretaceous period was fairly mild. Many modern plants developed, including those with flowers. With flowering plants came a greater diversity of insect life. Birds further developed into two types: flying and flightless. Prehistoric creatures such as *Ankylosaurus, Edmontosaurus, Iguanodon, Maiasaura, Oviraptor, Psittacosaurus, Spinosaurus, Triceratops, Troodon, Tyrannosaurus rex,* and *Velociraptor* all existed during this period. At the end of the Cretaceous period came a great mass extinction that wiped out the dinosaurs, along with many other groups of animals.

TERTIARY PERIOD

Date: 65 million to 1.8 million years ago

Mammals were extremely diversified at this time, and modern-day creatures such as horses, dogs, cats, bears, and whales developed.

QUATERNARY PERIOD

Date: 1.8 million years ago to today

Temperatures continued to drop during this period. Several periods of glacial development led to what is known as the Ice Age. Prehistoric creatures such as glyptodonts, mammoths, mastodons, *Megatherium,* and saber-toothed cats roamed Earth. A mass extinction of these animals occurred approximately 10,000 years ago. The first human beings evolved during the Quaternary period.

Index

About the Author

Susan H. Gray has bachelor's and master's degrees in zoology and has taught college-level courses in biology. She first fell in love with fossil hunting while studying paleontology in college. In her 25 years as an author, she has written many articles for scientists and researchers, and many science books for children. Susan enjoys gardening, traveling, and playing the piano. She and her husband, Michael, live in Cabot, Arkansas.